CLAY, WOOD and WIRE

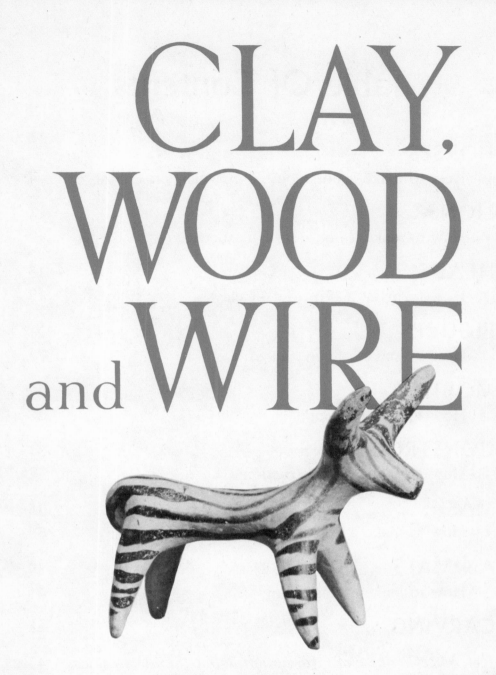

A HOW-TO-DO-IT BOOK OF SCULPTURE

By Harvey Weiss

NEW YORK: WILLIAM R. SCOTT, INC., PUBLISHER

Table Of Contents

Thanks and acknowledgment are due the following museums, institutions, and individuals for their cooperation and generous help in the preparation of this book: The Museum of Modern Art, New York; The American Museum of Natural History, New York; The Metropolitan Museum of Art, New York; The Rhode Island School of Design Museum, Providence, Rhode Island; The Cleveland Art Institute, Cleveland, Ohio; The Boston Museum of Fine Arts, Boston, Massachusetts; The Old Dartmouth Historical and Whaling Museum, New Bedford, Massachusetts; Soprintendenza Antichita, Firenze, Italy; Washington University, St. Louis, Missouri; The Des Moines Art Center, Des Moines, Iowa; The Canadian Department of Northern Affairs and National Resources, Ottawa; Mr. Bert Beaver; Miss Dorothea Denislow of the Sculpture Center, New York; Mr. Glen Chamberlain; Miss Kate Bernhardt; May, Bill, John, and especially my wife, Miriam.

This is a book about sculpture. It's about how to make lions, and horses, and heads, and figures running, and designs that can hang and twirl. It's about pipe-cleaners, and clay, and cardboard, and plasticene, and plaster. It's about all sorts of things that are easy to make if you know how to go about it.

It shows you how other people have made sculpture, and it will show you how to get started making your own sculpture out of many different materials.

b.

c.

d.

e.

f.

g.

HORSES

Here are horses—six of them—galloping, prancing, or just standing still. Some are small and simple, some are big and complicated. They are six horses made the way six different artists felt like making a horse. No one horse is more "right" or "correct" than any other. They are just different. They are different because each artist had his own special feeling about a horse. But notice that even the ones that are very simple and uncomplicated have the lively, prancing, galloping feeling of a horse.

What's your way to make a horse? How would you do it? Do you like the nice thin legs? Or would you concentrate on the big round, galloping body with a long neck and a flowing mane? Or maybe you're especially fond of lazy horses munching grass or a horse prancing in a parade.

These are things for you to decide, because now *you're* the artist.

The next few pages show you how to make a horse out of a material that's very easy to manage. With pipe-cleaners it's the easiest thing in the world. Here's how you do it . . .

h.

i.

6

How To Make A Horse Out Of Pipe-Cleaners

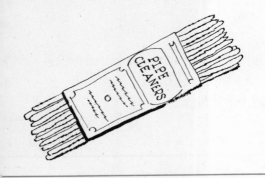

1. The first thing you need is a handful of pipe-cleaners. You can get them in any cigar store, or, if you know someone who smokes a pipe, he'll have some.

2. Make the hind legs first. Just take one cleaner and bend it in the middle.

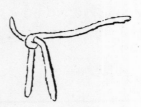

3. Now take another cleaner and twist it around the hind legs. Let a little bit stick out for the tail.

4. Twist on another cleaner for the front legs. Then put on another for the neck and head.

5. Cut off a small piece and wrap it around the head. If you let the ends stick up a little, you will have the ears. At this point the horse can stand on its own four feet and should begin to look something like a horse. Now is the time for you to decide just how you want it to look—fat, skinny, tired, galloping, sitting, munching lunch? That's up to you. It's your horse.

6. If you want the body a little fatter, take more pipe-cleaners and wrap them around the body between the front and back legs.

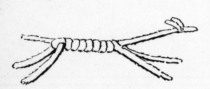

7. One of the nice things about making your horse out of pipe-cleaners is that, once he's all put together, you can try different things with him. Try spreading his feet apart and see if you can make him look as if he's running fast. Make the head and neck stretch forward, and he'll look as if he were really dashing along. Notice how the straight line of the back and the neck helps to give him a feeling of speed.

8. See if you can make your horse have the feeling of trotting. Then his neck will be up, straight and proud. How about lifting one of his feet up in the air and making his tail stick up? He'll seem to prance along.

9. Maybe you'd like to put a rider on his back. If you do, you'll need four more pipe-cleaners. Take one and bend it in the middle. This will be the legs.

10. Take another and bend the top a half-inch down. This will be the head and body. Fasten it to the legs.

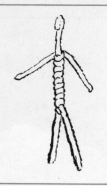

11. Twist on another piece, just below the head, for the arms. And wrap still another around the body to make it a little heavier.

12. Put the man on the horse's back. If the horse is racing, you'll probably want the rider leaning forward, holding the reins. (You can make the reins out of some heavy thread.)

13. There are lots of things you can do with your horse and rider. See what other actions you can discover. Don't be afraid to bend and twist and turn and experiment. When you decide that you're all finished, you can cut out a piece of cardboard and cement the horse's feet to it. This will be the base and will keep the horse from being knocked over.

You can make all sorts of other animals or figures out of pipe-cleaners. What about a dinosaur? Or two people running? Or a big-eared donkey pulling a wagon? Or a leopard? (You can paint spots on him.) Or a giraffe with a long thin neck? Or an octopus with twelve arms all painted black? You can make a whole zoo full of animals, or a farm, or a rodeo of cowpunchers with lassos. It's up to you.

a.

b.

c.

LIONS

Lions are fun to make. Look at these. They're strong and exciting and handsome. They have a fierce, king-of-the-jungle look.

They don't all look exactly like the lions you see in the zoo, but these are *sculpture*-lions. A sculpture lion can give the *feeling* of a real lion, even if he doesn't look too much like a real lion. Sometimes just a few lumps of clay put together in the right way will do the trick. You can suggest the roar without every whisker being there. A statue doesn't have to be fussy or real-looking to get the feeling of a lion.

You can make a lion. It's not much harder than the horse.

What do you want your lion to look like? Do you want him to look fierce? Maybe you'd prefer a friendly little baby lion to a fierce roaring one. Or maybe your fierce lion will end up looking more like a house cat or a shaggy poodle. In that case there's no reason why you can't just pretend that's what you wanted to make in the first place! (Nobody will ever know.)

You can't always get just what you want the first time you try, but if *you* like the way it comes out—then you're doing all right.

How To Make A Lion Out Of Plasticene

1. First get some plasticene. (You can get it in any art store.) Plasticene is a kind of clay that never dries up. It is strong and easy to manage, and you can use it over and over again.

2. To start your lion, you need a flat piece of wood for a base. A heavy piece of cardboard will do if you can't get wood. About 4 x 6 inches is a good size.

3. Make four balls of plasticene. These will be the legs. You'll find that the plasticene is hard and stiff if you use big lumps of it, but if you break off little pieces and squeeze them in your fingers a few times they will become soft and workable.

4. Make another, larger, longer ball and put it on top of the four legs. This will be the body. Make sure the legs are squeezed firmly into the body.

5. Then make another large oval ball for the head. Squeeze it on good and tight, or it may fall off later.

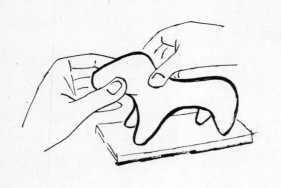

6. Here the fun begins. You have somewhat the shape of a lion. Now push and poke and squeeze and pinch. Add plasticene or take it away. Keep at it until your lion begins to look the way you want it to. Be bold. Get the graceful "sweep" of the back. Get the powerful, round chest and big, proud head. At first it may not look like a lion to anyone but you. But take your time about it, and keep trying until you begin to get what you want.

7. You are making a lion, and the thing about lions is that they roar. So let's make him roar. Just scoop out a big mouth. Put in his teeth. Now is he roaring? If you were making a hippopotamus instead of a lion, you would make him big and round and lumpy and heavy. If you were making a snake, you would make him thin and wriggly and squiggly. If you were making a wart hog, you would make him wrinkled and bumpy and warty and ugly. Every animal has some one special thing you will want to emphasize.

8. Last of all put in the smaller details, like eyes and ears and paws and tail. You can make the eyes just by poking a couple of holes in the head with the point of a pencil. A little ball of plasticene can make the nose. You can make the lion's mane with thin strips of plasticene stuck on, one on top of the other, all around the head.

9. When you think you're through with your lion, try holding him up against a strong light and look to see if he has a clean, definite outline or silhouette. Look at him from all sides. If he is bumpy and unsure, work on him some more.

If you feel that you would rather make your lion some other way—do it. Maybe you would rather have him sitting down, or yawning, or all curled up sleeping.

Or maybe you'd rather make an elephant, or an airplane, or a tugboat, or a kangaroo with a baby in its pouch, or a tiny mouse with big ears and a long tail.

If you like, you can make the lion out of clay instead of plasticene. But if you do, read the next chapter first, so you will know how to handle the clay.

a.

d.

c.

b.

e.

h.

HEADS

Big eyes or little eyes? Curly hair, big chin, pointy chin, small ears, stubby nose or long nose? That's what heads are made of, and that's what makes one head different from another.

Sometimes just a few scratches in the clay will suggest these things and give the whole feeling and mood of a head.

Look at that fellow above and to the left. He's made up of a few simple shapes, but they tell a lot. One hand is raised to his head. His eyes are big and startled. He could be about to say, "Oh, what an awful headache I've got," or, "Gosh, why didn't I think of that!"

Some of these heads look like someone in particular, and are called "portraits." Others are just for fun. Maybe the artist felt like making a head with big ears and a fancy hat. Or maybe he decided he would make a head with round smooth shapes that are nice to touch. Perhaps he wanted to show how happy a friend looks when he laughs.

Sometimes a dot with a sharp tool will look like an eye, or a lump of clay will make a nose. A line scratched in the clay can make a fine mouth.

g.

i.

j.

k.

How To Make A Head Out Of Clay

Clay is used for sculpture more often than any other material. You can squeeze and push and form it like plasticene, but, when it dries, it is quite hard. If you want it still harder, you can bake it in a special, very hot oven called a "kiln." This baking is called "firing." After it is fired, the clay is called "terra cotta," which is Latin for "cooked earth." Special colors, called "glazes," can be baked onto the clay, or it can be painted with ordinary paints.

Many schools have kilns for firing clay. And potters and brickmakers also have kilns. If you ask around in your neighborhood, the chances are you'll find there's a kiln nearby where you can take your finished things to be fired.

Another possibility is to use one of the special clays which can be fired in a kitchen oven. And then there is still another kind of clay, called "self-hardening," which dries hard as a rock without any firing at all.

But even if you can't locate a kiln or get these special clays, regular clay is all right. You'll just have to handle the finished pieces a little more gently.

1. To start making a head get some clay from an art store. Find a small square board and put a nail in the center of it. This will keep the clay from falling over.

2. Then squeeze and squish the clay until it is easy to handle. (This will also work out the air bubbles that would cause trouble later if you are going to fire your piece.) If the clay seems too stiff and hard, or if it cracks when you bend it, it is probably too dry. Sprinkle a little water on it.

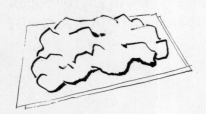

3. If the clay is soft and mushy, it is too wet. Spread it out on a newspaper for a few minutes and let it dry a bit.

17

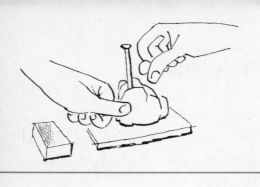

4. Start by putting clay, bit by bit, around and above the nail. Slowly and carefully build up the shape you want. Concentrate on getting the rough general shape of the head first.

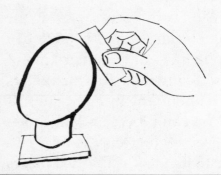

5. Most people's heads are shaped like an egg, but make the head the way you want it. Maybe you want a square head or a perfectly round one. Whatever you do, make it a definite shape, not a wishy-washy one. A block of wood is a handy tool to use for "tapping" the clay into the shapes you want.

6. When you are satisfied with the shape of the head, *then* start on the details like eyes, mouth, hair. You may be able to "pinch out" some of these shapes from the larger mass.

7. The mouth can be a simple straight line scratched under the nose. The eyes can be a couple of large dots, and a little roll of clay placed above them will make the eyebrows.

8. Two small flaps of clay will make the ears. And the hair will look best if you try to get the rough general shapes rather than a lot of tiny, scratchy strands of hair.

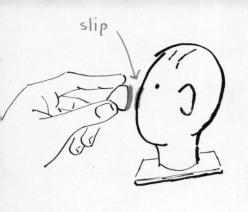

slip

9. You may find it easier to add on separate parts like nose, or ears, or a hat. When you add separate parts, first take a little clay and water and mix them until the clay becomes quite mushy. This mushy clay is called "slip," and it will act as a sort of cement that will help the parts stick together. Whenever you want to join two pieces of clay, spread a layer of slip over both parts where they join. Then squeeze them together hard. If you don't, they may fall apart when the clay dries out.

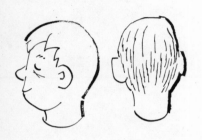

10. Keep turning the head around as you work on it, so that you see it from all sides. Keep the parts simple and forget about all the little bumps and wrinkles and freckles.

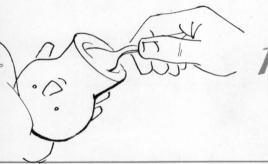

11. When the head is finished you can take it off the wooden base. If you turn it upside down and scoop out some of the clay from the inside with a spoon or a wire tool, it will be easier to fire.

12. After the clay is completely dry, it can be painted or fired.

Try making different kinds of heads. You can make an old man in a hat, a little girl with lots of curly hair. Or how about the head of a dog, or a cat, or a rhinoceros?

If the head you make doesn't look like any of the pictures in the book, never mind. It shouldn't. Everybody makes things his own way. If *you* like it, it's good!

a.

b.

c.

d.

20

e.

FIGURES

Here are figures that were made in many places and in many different times. That fellow playing the harp was made by an artist on an island in the Mediterranean four thousand years before Columbus discovered America. The dancers were made in France only forty or fifty years ago. The sad-looking man holding his head was found in Mexico. Nobody knows for sure just when it was made.

But all these figures have one thing in common. They are simple and they are bold. In the figure that you make, this is the thing to try for.

Look at how strong that Eskimo is! He's just a few simple, round shapes, and yet he really looks as if he's tugging away.

And the two men running—there's nothing fussy or tricky about them. They just have the bouncy, stretching feeling of running.

Making a figure out of clay is a little more difficult than making a head. But, if you take your time and follow the directions, it should turn out the way you want it to.

Here's how to do it.

k.

g.　　　　h.　　　　i.　　　　j.

l.

m.

n.

o.

p.

How To Make A Figure

1. One way of making a figure is by putting together balls of clay—a big one for the body, a small round one for the head, four long ones for the arms and legs. This is very much like the way you put the plasticene lion together, earlier in the book.

2. Another good way to start is with a "stick figure." It's the same sort of figure you can draw with a pencil or crayon on paper, only now you're using clay. Make rolls of clay and put them together in the shape of a figure. Be sure that all the parts are joined firmly together. This is important. Use a little very mushy clay ("slip") as a cement and squeeze the parts hard into one another.

3. Now, decide just what kind of figure you want to make. Experiment with the stick figure. Try shifting and twisting and bending it in different positions until you find one you like. (If you make your figure sitting or kneeling or lying down it will be much easier.)

4. If you decide you want to make a clown standing with his hands on his hips, for example, this is what you do. Get a piece of wood for a base and press the feet onto it. Try to make the figure stand up by itself. If you made the clay rolls too thin, you will find that the figure will sag. In that case, add more clay, bit by bit, until it stands up by itself. You'll probably have to make very thick and heavy legs. Always bear in mind that clay is *not* a good material for making light, thin shapes. They are sure to break off when the clay dries out.

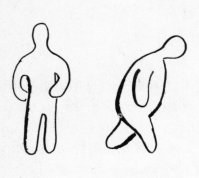

5. After you have your clown standing up, add more clay, a piece at a time, getting the shapes just the way you want them. Keep thinking of how you want the clown to look. If you make shapes that are straight and bold and strong, then the clown will have the feeling of strength and boldness. If you make shapes that are bent-over and droopy and sad, then your clown will look droopy and sad. The way you shape the clay will give your clown his own special look.

6. Try twisting his head in different directions. You can make him look up, down, or to the side. And how about his arms? There are many different ways to place them besides on the hips. And his legs—they can be bent, straight, twisted, spread apart, bowlegged, or even knock-kneed.

7. After you have all the big main shapes in place, put in the details. Don't put in so many that the figure is all cluttered up. Try a big nose that you can paint a bright red when the clay is dried out or fired. How about a funny hat? And what about great big, floppy shoes?

8. If you want to get a slightly different look in some places, try scratching or scraping the clay with a knife or a modeling tool. Or roll up little balls of clay and press them into place.

Try making some other figures. How about an acrobat standing on his head? Or a figure about to throw a basketball? Or two people wrestling? Or you might want to try making a figure by starting with a solid lump of clay and then taking away pieces until you get the figure you want. This is really a sort of carving.

Building A Figure On An Armature

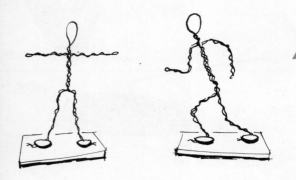

1. If you want to make a figure that isn't blocky and solid-looking, you would do better to use plasticene instead of clay. Use it over some kind of skeleton or "armature." An armature will keep the figure from falling over. You can make one out of soft copper wire, nailed or thumb-tacked to the base. Make the armature like a stick figure. Adjust it to the position you want. Then fasten it to the base.

2. Put the plasticene on, bit by bit, over the wire. Build up the shapes you want in the same way as with clay.

3. You can make a wire armature for animals as well as for figures. It's a little like making the horse out of pipe-cleaners, except that now you're using copper wire. If you are going to make a giraffe, for example, the best way to keep the long, long thin neck and spindly legs from collapsing is to use an armature. It's up to you to decide when you need an armature.

MOBILES

A sculpture that moves is called a "mobile." A mobile is a combination of carefully-balanced shapes that hang from the ceiling. The slightest draft will set them spinning and turning and jiggling. As the mobile moves, its different parts move into different designs. It is always changing.

A mobile isn't usually made to look like anything in life. You are not apt to make mobiles that look like faces or figures, although you could. Instead, the interesting thing about mobiles is their design, their ever-changing quality, and the shadows that they cast.

The old Greek and Roman sculptors never heard of a mobile. In fact, nobody did until twenty or thirty years ago. It's a new type of sculpture that was first made by an American artist by the name of Alexander Calder.

All you need in order to make one are some pieces of cardboard, some stiff wire, a pair of pliers, and some string.

b.

How To Make A Mobile

The important thing about a mobile is to make it hang so that it balances. This isn't as easy as it looks.

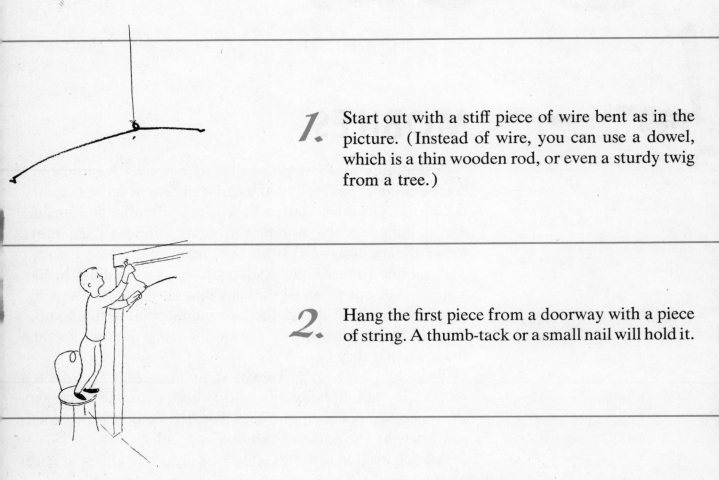

1. Start out with a stiff piece of wire bent as in the picture. (Instead of wire, you can use a dowel, which is a thin wooden rod, or even a sturdy twig from a tree.)

2. Hang the first piece from a doorway with a piece of string. A thumb-tack or a small nail will hold it.

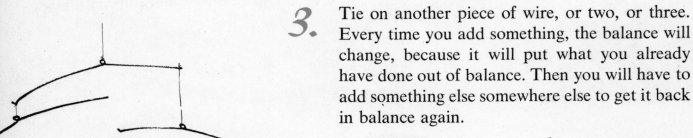

3. Tie on another piece of wire, or two, or three. Every time you add something, the balance will change, because it will put what you already have done out of balance. Then you will have to add something else somewhere else to get it back in balance again.

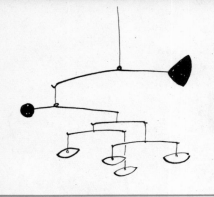

4. Try cutting cardboard into shapes you like, painting them, and then tieing them on.

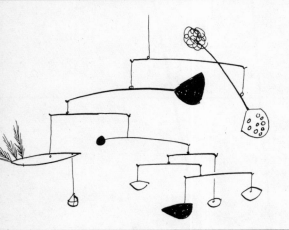

5. Feathers are fun to put on. And what about pebbles, or cellophane in bright colors, paper clips, ribbons? Almost anything light in weight can be put on a mobile. But before you add everything in sight, stop to think how it will look. Too little is often better than too much.

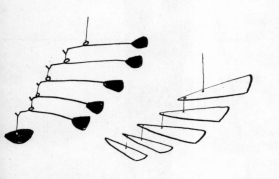

6. Try different types and combinations of balancing, and don't get discouraged if you have to do it over and over until you get it just right. If there is a part you don't like, then take it off and make something different to go in its place.

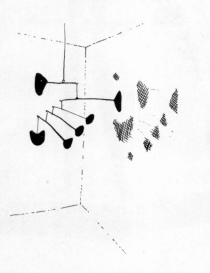

7. When you are satisfied that your mobile is as handsome as you can make it, then hang it from the ceiling in the middle of your room. You can tie it to a light fixture, for example, or tack it to the top of a window or doorway—any place where it can hang freely will do. Watch it move. Blow at it and see how it swings. Notice the shadows that it casts. That's half the fun.

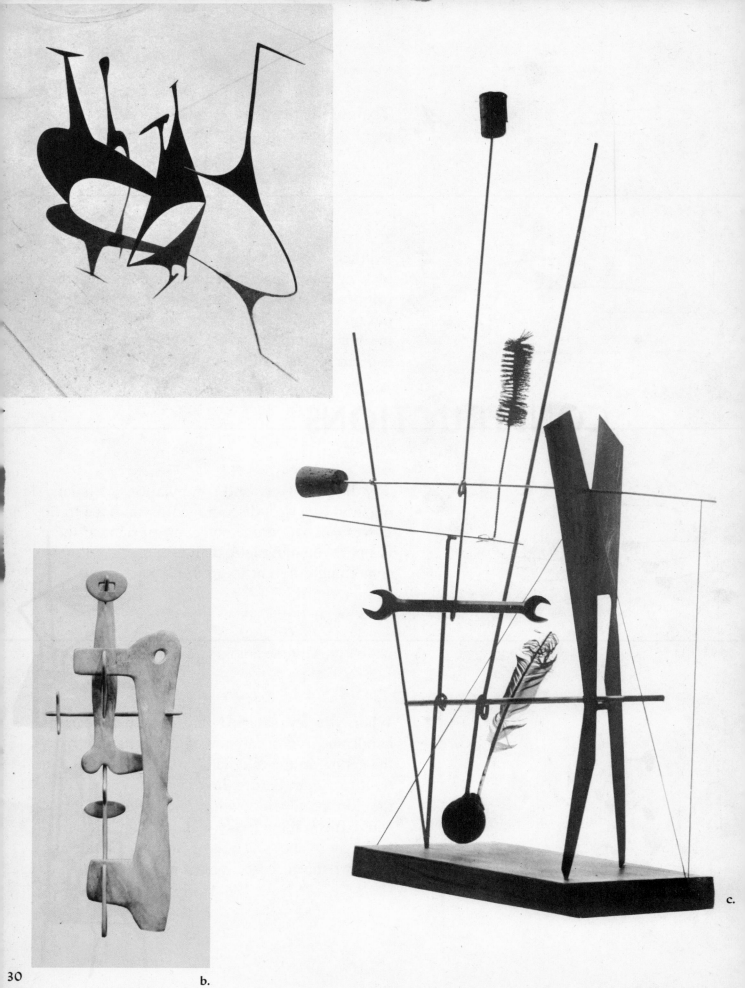

b.

c.

d.

CONSTRUCTIONS

STABILES

A construction is just like a mobile, except that it sits on a base and doesn't hang. It can have moving parts, or everything can be tied firmly in place. It can be made of one material like cardboard, or wire, or rods. Or, like the big one on the opposite page, it can be a combination of all kinds of different things.

Just a plain piece of wood sticking out of a base would be pretty boring to look at. But if there's another piece of wood tied to it, it becomes a little more interesting. Let a few objects dangle from the stick, paint on some color, tie or tack on a variety of different things, and it can become really exciting to look at. And that's what a construction is—a putting together of all sorts of different shapes and materials.

Look at the constructions on these pages. Notice how the shapes are chosen and combined to make a lively, varied design. And look at the empty spaces *between* the shapes. After all, they are a part of the design too.

There are no rules for making a construction. Actually there are no rules for any kind of art. In art, you are your own boss. What you like is what is right!

e.

How To Make A Construction

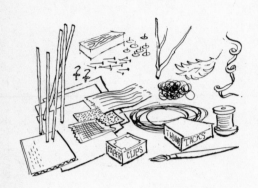

1. Get some cardboard, some thin wooden rods (dowels), or twigs, or wire. Get a piece of corrugated cardboard for a base. See if you can find some interesting-looking objects like colored paper, or leaves, or scraps of wood, or odds and ends of any kind. Try to find materials with different kinds of feeling or "texture," like bits of silk, sandpaper, steel wool, or bark. And you will probably need some string or thin wire.

2. Start by cutting out some cardboard shapes. Paint them. You may want to cut holes or spaces in them.

3. Try cutting little slots in the cardboard shapes and fitting one into another.

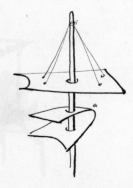

4. Poke the wire or twigs or dowels through the holes in the cardboard. Tie them in place where necessary.

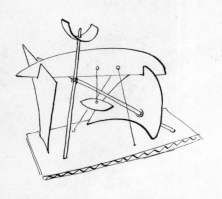

5. Now combine some of these things in as interesting and lively a design as possible. (You don't have to use everything.) See what shapes look well together, and what colors look well next to one another.

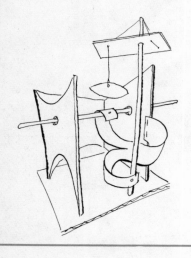

6. Try gluing on different things, or let some objects dangle from a string. If there is a stapler around, you can use that for fastening things together.

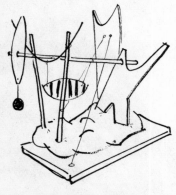

7. If you have trouble getting everything to stand up in place, use a lump of clay as a base and stick things into that.

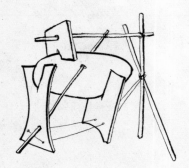

8. Keep turning your construction as you work on it. See how it looks from all sides. Make sure it's not a jumble.

MASKS

These masks are a special kind of sculpture. They were made not as objects of art but as something to be used in tribal ceremonies or religious dances or dramatic performances.

They are supposed to look like powerful gods or protective spirits. That's why they rarely look like a real face. If the protective spirit was thought to look like some kind of animal, the mask was made to look like that animal, and the chief medicine man or witch doctor would wear it or dance in it while praying for special favors from that particular spirit. They are fierce and fanciful—sometimes even frightening.

Masks are often decorated with beads and feathers and usually painted in red, brown, black, and white.

A wooden mask is terribly heavy and uncomfortable to wear, but a papier-mâché mask is light and easy to wear or fun to hang up on a wall. It can be wild and ferocious, or funny, or sad. It can be like a clown, like an animal, like anything in the world—or like anything that *isn't* in the world! The more fantastic the better.

b.

c.

d.

e.

f.

g.

35

How To Make A Mask Out Of Papier-Mâché

1. To make a mask you'll need some clay, some newspapers, and some paper-hanger's paste. You can get the paste at any paint or hardware store. The mask will have to be started one day and finished off a few days later, because it has to dry for several days before it hardens and can be painted.

2. The first step is to make the shape of the mask roughly in clay. Let your imagination run free—the more fanciful the better.

3. Get some newspapers and rip them into long thin strips. About an inch wide is good.

4. Fill a small bowl half-full of water. Mix the paste into the water until the mixture begins to get thick and gooey.

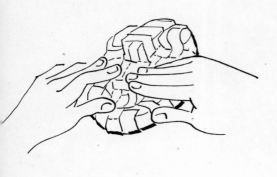

5. Then dip the strips into the paste, one at a time, and place them over the clay. Keep adding one strip over the other, criss-crossing them. Press each strip down and smooth it so that there are no air bubbles caught under the paper. If the paper gets too wet and mushy put on a dry strip now and then.

6. Keep adding more strips until you have twenty or thirty layers of paper over the clay. Shape the soggy paper with your fingers until you have the exact shapes that you want. Then put it aside and let it dry for several days. When it does dry, it will be hard and quite strong.

7. After the mask is dry, turn it upside down and take out the clay. Trim the edges of the paper with a heavy pair of scissors. Drill a hole in each side, so that you can attach a string. If you want to wear the mask, cut out the eyes.

8. Paint it. Then glue on feathers or beads or long shreds of paper, or whatever else you feel like.

9. You can make several bird and animal masks, hang or fasten one above the other, and you have a totem pole!

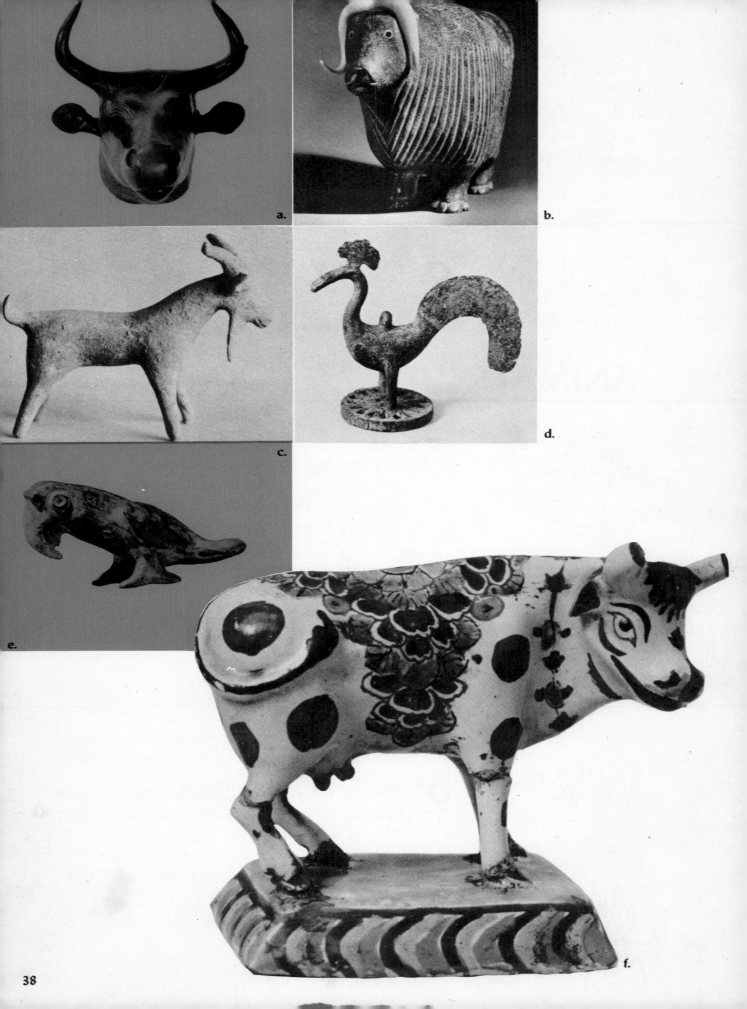

a.

b.

c.

d.

e.

f.

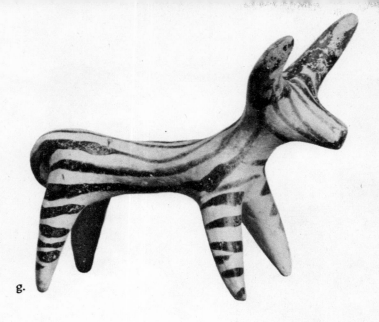

g.

ANIMALS

You'd have to look a long, long time before you'd find a real cow with a bunch of flowers painted on its side, but when it comes to a *sculpture*-cow anything can happen!

The sculptor who made that cow on the left just felt like painting flowers on its side, so he went ahead and did, and it looks just fine.

The sculptor who made the peacock liked the nice sweep of the tail, so he just concentrated on that and didn't even bother with the other things like feathers and wings and claws.

The artist who made the funny animal at the top of this page decided that stripes would look well on it, even though it isn't a tiger or a zebra. So he just went ahead and put them on.

This is one of the nicest things about any kind of art—you're free to do what you like. If you think something will look well, there's nothing in the world to keep you from trying it!

h.

i.

j.

How To Make A Plaster Cow

Plaster is a hard white material that is easy to paint, although it's tricky to handle. Lots of things look well in plaster—a cow, or a bull, or a polar bear—anything big and bulky. If you want to make a cow, for example, this is how you do it.

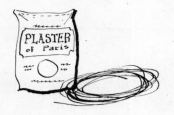

1. Get a big roll of thin, galvanized iron wire and a small bag of plaster of Paris. You can get them in any hardware store.

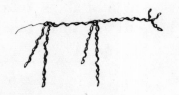

2. Start by making a simple skeleton or "armature" for the cow in the same way you made the horse out of pipe-cleaners earlier in the book.

3. Make sure the legs and neck aren't wobbly. Then wrap the wire around and around the armature, so that the shapes get a little stronger and bulkier. Wrap the wire on good and tight, and don't be afraid to use plenty of it. Wrap lots and lots of it on, until the cow begins to look fat. Try to get the lazy, saggy feeling of a cow.

4. When you're satisfied with the shape and pose of the cow, put it aside and mix your plaster. Follow these directions *exactly,* if you want the plaster to dry hard and strong. Get an old china cup. Fill it half full of water. *Slowly* sprinkle the plaster into the water without stirring, until the plaster fills up half the cup and absorbs all the water. <u>Sixteen level teaspoons in half a cup of water</u> is about right.

5. After you have the right amount of plaster in the water let it stand for half a minute. *Then* stir until the plaster is smooth and without lumps.

6. Now dip the cow, a part at a time, into the plaster. This will fill up all the little spaces between the wire.

7. As the plaster begins to get thick and gooey, pick up some more with a dull knife and spread it on, building up the shapes you want. The plaster will get hard and unworkable in about four or five minutes, so you have to mix small batches and work fast.

8. When the plaster in the cup gets too hard to manage throw it out and mix another batch. Be sure the cup is cleaned thoroughly between each batch.

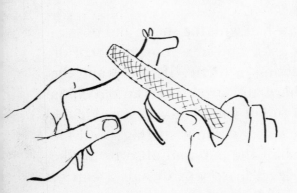

9. When you are finished, let the plaster dry for a day or two. Then, if you want, you can finish the surface with a file and sandpaper, or you can even whittle it with a knife. If you made the legs long and thin, you will have to work on them very carefully or they are apt to crack. Finally paint it. (Any kind of paint will do.)

Making A Bigger Plaster Cow

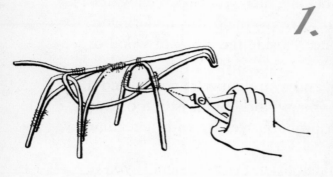

1. If you want to make a big cow, or some other big animal (and you may want to try making something good and big now), you'll have to make your armature a little differently because it will have to be stronger. Get some heavy, stiff wire and a pair of pliers. Build your armature out of this wire, using string or thin copper wire to tie the parts together. This is the most difficult part, so take your time and work slowly and carefully.

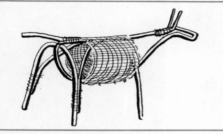

2. Cover the big, bulky places like the body with pieces of window screening. You can tie the pieces of screening in place with the thin wire.

3. Make this armature as neat and as strong as you can. Make sure everything is just the way you want it, because it is very hard to make changes once the plaster is hard. Cut up strips of burlap. Mix up some more plaster of Paris. Dip the strips of burlap into the plaster and wind them around the armature.

4. When the armature is completely covered with burlap, you can start to build up over it with the plaster. Then you can finish and paint it in the same way as you did the small cow.

Try making a figure in plaster—an acrobat hanging from a trapeze, or a boy and a girl on a see-saw, or a polar bear.

Wood Carving

If you've ever whittled a piece of wood with a penknife, or if you've even cut a piece of clay or plaster off of where it didn't belong, then you've carved. Carving is simply the process of removing material to get to the forms underneath. First you have to imagine the statue "imprisoned" inside the block of wood or stone, and then it's your job to release it!

Wood is easy to carve. You'll need a gouge, and a straight-edge chisel, and a mallet to hammer with. If the piece of wood you're working on isn't too hard (pine or oak are good) or too big, you can probably get by with a regular penknife.

Look at the grain of the wood and try to make it fit into your design. If you're making something large, put the wood in a vise so that it won't slide around as you work.

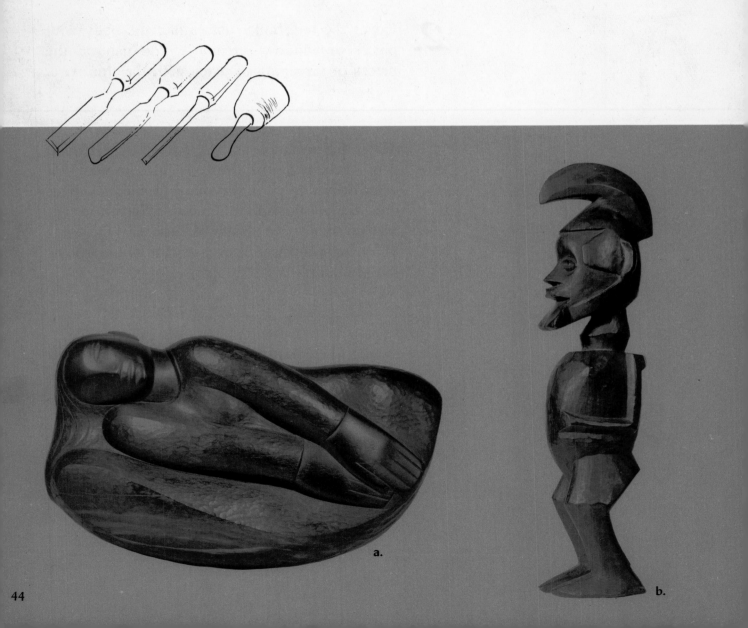

a.

b.

c.

d.

Stone Carving

The first sculptures ever made were done in the time of the cave man, and they were carved out of stone.

If you find a piece of stone that's not too hard, and if you feel like working slowly and carefully, you can carve it with steel chisels like the ones shown.

You'll have to make your design fit the stone, and you'll have to avoid sharp projections, which are difficult to carve and likely to break off. When you work, be sure to wear sun glasses or safety goggles to keep chips from flying into your eyes.

In both stone and wood, the simpler and more compact forms like fishes, or birds, or lumpy, fat figures are easiest to start with.

q.

Now you know the simple, basic ways of handling the materials of sculpture. You've seen the way the Indians and Egyptians and Etruscans and many others have used these materials to express their ideas and feelings.

But the things you've made, and the things you will go on to make are different, because sculpture, like any other art, is always an individual and a personal matter. The way you feel about something, what you see, what you make is yours and yours alone. If others see what you've done and like it—so much the better. But don't worry about pleasing other people. Please yourself first!

Don't be afraid to try out your own ideas. Don't hesitate to make your own discoveries. Now you're on your own.

OTHER BOOKS ON SCULPTURE

ZORACH EXPLAINS SCULPTURE, by William Zorach, American Artists Group.

SCULPTURE INSIDE AND OUT, by Malvina Hoffman, W. W. Norton and Co.

THE SCULPTOR'S WAY, by Brenda Putnam, Farrar and Rinehart.

SCULPTURE; PRINCIPLES AND PRACTICE, by Louis Slobodkin, World Publishing Company.

THE MATERIALS AND METHODS OF SCULPTURE, by Jack Rich, Oxford University Press.

ABOUT THE ILLUSTRATIONS

HORSES

a. HORSE, bronze, by Leonardo Da Vinci, Metropolitan Museum of Art. b. HORSE, bronze, by Edgar Degas, Metropolitan Museum of Art. c. MAN ON HORSE, terra cotta, Cypriote (1000-600 B.C.), Metropolitan Museum of Art. d. HORSE AND RIDER, bronze, by Marino Marini, Museum of Modern Art. e. HORSE AND RIDER, aquamanile, North European XIV Century, Metropolitan Museum of Art (Cloisters Collection). f. HORSE, bronze, archaic, American Museum of Natural History. g. HORSE, bronze, Greek VIII Century B.C., Metropolitan Museum of Art. h. HORSE, bronze, Greek V Century B.C., Metropolitan Museum of Art. i. HAUT ECOLE, bronze, by Amory C. Simons, Metropolitan Museum of Art.

LIONS

a. HEAD OF A LION (detail from a chimaera), bronze, Etruscan, Archaeological Museum, Florence, Italy. b. SEATED LION, stone, Chinese (Tang Period), Metropolitan Museum of Art. c. LION, terra cotta, by the author. d. LION, limestone, Egyptian, Metropolitan Museum of Art. e. LION SEATED, bronze, Greek VI Century B.C. f. HEAD OF A LION, marble, Greek V Century B.C.

HEADS

a. HEAD, bronze, Nigeria, Africa, American Museum of Natural History. b. FIGURINE (detail), terra cotta, probably Vera Cruz, Mexico, American Museum of Natural History. c. HEAD, terra cotta, Cypriote, Metropolitan Museum of Art. d. SEATED BISHOP (detail), polychromed wood, Flemish XIII Century, Cleveland Museum of Art, gift of John D. Rockefeller, Jr. e. HEAD, marble, Roman copy of a Greek head, Metropolitan Museum of Art. f. FIGURE (detail), terra cotta, Queretaro, Mexico, American Museum of Natural History. g. QUEEN HAT-SHEP-SUT, granite, Egypt XVIII Dynasty, about 1485 B.C., Metropolitan Museum of Art. h. CARVED STONE, Queriquerins Island, Bay of Conception, Chile, American Museum of Natural History. i. HEAD, stone, Easter Islands, American Museum of Natural History. j. HEAD OF BUDDHA, bronze, Indian, author's collection. k. HEAD, terra cotta, Cypriote VII Century B.C., Metropolitan Museum of Art. l. MADONNA AND CHILD (detail), oak, Eastern French or Flemish, Cleveland Museum of Art, gift of John D. Rockefeller, Jr.

FIGURES

a. MAN WITH A HARP, marble, Cycladic 2500 B.C., Metropolitan Museum of Art. b. THE RUNNERS, bronze, by Gerhard Marcks, Museum of Modern Art, gift of Mrs. John D. Rockefeller, Jr. c. SEATED FIGURE, terra cotta, archaic culture, Mexico, American Museum of Natural History. d. ESKIMO CARVING, stone, by an unknown Eskimo artist from Port Harrison, Department of Northern Affairs and Natural Resources, Canada. e. f. g. h. i. j. DANCERS, bronze, by Edgar Degas, Metropolitan Museum of Art. k. NAVIGATOR, wood, Old Dartmouth Historical and Whaling Museum. l. WARRIOR, bronze, Etruscan, Metropolitan Museum of Art. m. WARRIOR WITH SPEAR, terra cotta, Tarascan, Mexico, Museum of Art of the Rhode Island School of Design. n. FIGURE, Tepic, Mexico, American Museum of Natural History. o. ACROBATS, plaster, by the author. p. RECLINING FIGURE, cast stone, by Henry Moore, Washington University Art Collection. q. (page 46) "WELL, SO LONG NOW," plaster, by the author, collection of the publisher.

MOBILES

a. BLACK SPREAD, metal and wire, by Alexander Calder, Des Moines Art Center, Edmundson Collection. b. GAD-ABOUT, wire, cardboard, pebbles, brush, and typewriter erasers, by the author.

CONSTRUCTIONS

a. SPINY, aluminum, by Alexander Calder, Private Collection, New York. b. KOUROS, marble, by Isamu Noguchi, Metropolitan Museum of Art. c. NUTCRACKER-DUSTER, sheet-metal, feather, corks, wrench, wire, brush, by the author. d. THE PALACE AT 4 A.M., wood, glass, wire, string, by Alberto Giacometti, Museum of Modern Art. e. CITY LANDSCAPE, bronze, by the author.

MASKS

a. FACE PLATE FROM GABLE OF MEN'S HOUSE, wood, New Guinea, American Museum of Natural History. b. WOODEN MASK, Bampende Colony, Africa, American Museum of Natural History. c. DRAMATIC MASK, wood, Java, American Museum of Natural History. d. DANCING MASK, wood and dyed sage bark, New Guinea, American Museum of Natural History. e. MASK, wood and feathers, Alaska, American Museum of Natural History. f. ELEPHANT MASK, wood, Bampende Colony, Africa, American Museum of Natural History. g. DRAMATIC MASK, wood, Java, American Museum of Natural History.

ANIMALS

a. HEAD OF BULL, bronze, archaic Greek, American Museum of Natural History. b. MUSK-OX, stone, by Akeeaktashuk, Ellesmere Island, Canada, Collection of Mr. Bert Beaver. c. GOAT, terra cotta, archaic Greek, Metropolitan Museum of Art. d. PEACOCK, bronze, Greek VIII Century B.C., Metropolitan Museum of Art. e. PARROT, terra cotta, Colima style, Mexico, American Museum of Natural History. f. COW, Delft, Dutch 18th Century, Metropolitan Museum of Art. g. OX, terra cotta, Greek (about 1400-1100 B.C.), Metropolitan Museum of Art. h. FALCON, bronze, European (XII-XIII Century), Metropolitan Museum of Art, Cloisters Collection. i. STANDING BULL, bronze, by Elie Nadelman, Museum of Modern Art, gift of Mrs. Elie Nadelman. j. POLAR BEAR, stone, by Tikeetuk, Baffin Island, Canada, Collection of Mr. Bert Beaver.

CARVING

a. DANCER, wood, by Glen Chamberlain, Sculpture Center Gallery. b. FETISH FIGURE, wood, Africa, American Museum of Natural History. c. TRIUMPH OF THE EGG, I, granite, by John B. Flannagan, Museum of Modern Art. d. HEAD OF CHRIST, granite, by William Zorach, The Museum of Modern Art.

2/35

Jan 23. 55